# CROSSING THE FINISHING LINE

# Crossing
# the Finishing Line

## Last thoughts
## of Leonard Cheshire, VC

Edited by
Reginald C. Fuller

With a Foreword by
Bishop Alan C. Clark

ST PAULS

Cover portrait by kind permission of the artist, June Mendoza.

ST PAULS
Morpeth Terrace, London SW1P 1EP, United Kingdom
Maynooth, Co. Kildare, Ireland

© ST PAULS (UK) 1998

ISBN 085439 527 X

Set by TuKan, High Wycombe
Produced in the EU
Printed by The Guernsey Press Co. Ltd, Guernsey, C.I.

ST PAULS is an activity of the priests and brothers of the
Society of St Paul who proclaim the Gospel through the media
of social communication

# Contents

Foreword 7

Introduction 11

I  Coming to Terms with Illness,
   June 1992 15

II  The Family of the Cross
    Reflections, June 1992 27

III  Leave-taking, July 1992 65

Epilogue 80

# Foreword

It is only rarely that even close friends are allowed to enter into the prayer-filled thoughts of a dying man of the calibre of Leonard Cheshire. Fr Reginald Fuller has in the following precious pages put together these thoughts taken down in writing on different occasions by those who were 'with Leonard' in the last months of his life. He has carried out a difficult task. So many people who enjoyed the company and friendship of Leonard will feel privileged to read of his prayerful search and his 'finding' of the ways of God.

Of those with him in his last illness none

was closer than Sue (Lady Ryder of Warsaw) who, as wife and confidante, as well as nurse, was particularly united with him in that sacred part of his life – his going forth to God. He died at their home in Cavendish, Suffolk, known as the Sue Ryder Home, where they had spent all their married life when not travelling abroad on behalf of their respective Foundations.

Leonard, as is well-known, suffered from motor neurone disease and in spite of the stress involved spoke of the truth as he experienced it. His 'conclusions' were hard-won which makes this booklet all the more valuable to those who, one way or another, knew him and enjoyed his friendship.

What follows then is a record of some of Leonard's deeply-held convictions which, even in the period of his sharply declining health, he wished to share with others. The title in Leonard's own words, (see p.37) and sub-title give only a faint idea of the profound intensity of his faith and spiritual experience. But the record here given is sufficient to reveal something of the mind and heart of a unique 'soul' full of grace and truth. One is overwhelmed by the greatness of his friendship with Christ at the centre of his being.

Our thanks go to Sue, his wife, to Fr Reginald Fuller and to all those who took part in making these *verba ipsissima* of Leonard Cheshire available to us.

*Alan C. Clark*
*Bishop Emeritus of East Anglia*

# Introduction

Group Captain Cheshire V.C., famous bomber-pilot and hero of World War II, was, in many ways, unique. His quiet, unassuming manner concealed a man of vision, of striking, even reckless bravery, and of quick decision. All this without a trace of religion, until after the war, when he was seeking some worthwhile purpose in life, something that would benefit humanity in place of causing destruction.

He discovered his solution in the founding of Homes for the disabled and, in the process, was converted to the Catholic Faith. The full story has yet to be told in the biography soon to appear. Here we offer a small but precious legacy; a record of conversations taken down during the last two months of his life in which he reveals, as Bishop Clark movingly points out in his Foreword, his dedication to the Lord he had at last found and who now claimed his total allegiance.

It is characteristic of Leonard Cheshire that in passing on these thoughts his one aim was that they might be of assistance to others in their own lives. Among those who kept him company during his last illness were priest-friends, including Augustinian Fathers from the neighbouring Priory at Clare, Suffolk.

These chapters should in no sense be regarded as a connected narrative, which would have been impossible anyway, given the state of his health. We have rather a series of reflections on matters that deeply concerned him, formed under conditions that would have defeated most people.

One is struck forcefully by the contrast between the action-packed life he had led and the constraints of the fatal motor neurone disease which steadily deprived him of his physical abilities. Such a situation would be traumatic in any age but perhaps most of all in the present-day world where physical health and material possessions are commonly regarded as essential to a worthwhile life. This was the challenge that Leonard had often to meet since World War II but now urgently on his 'last long journey', to use Freya Stark's graphic phrase. He met it, as always, head-on accepting in advance all that it implied. But, as the disease developed the implications of all that this involved were not absorbed without a struggle. He had not yet reached perfection, but with St Paul he pressed on, 'hoping to take hold of that for which Christ once took hold of me' (Phil 3:12).

In leaving us these 'thoughts', it was Cheshire's desire to offer the Family of the Cross (see p.27) some encouragement, derived mainly from his own experience both in founding the Homes and, more especially, during his last illness. The Family was founded to continue and develop the spiritual dimension to the work of the Homes. Some of his ideas may be found more fully discussed in the interview with Alenka Lawrence* and it was Leonard Cheshire's

* Leonard Cheshire, *Where is God in all this?* Interview by Alenka Lawrence, St Paul Publications, 1991

intention to develop these 'last thoughts' further if circumstances allowed; but death intervened. It has been thought best to set down what he had to say largely as spoken, even at the expense of some overlapping and discontinuity. Editorial work has consisted mainly of arranging material, clarifying passages where this was required and giving references to Scripture quotations. One or two footnotes have been added.

It will be noticed by the reader that, in spite of the debilitating nature of the sickness, his mental faculties remained intact to the end. This is how he preferred it even though it meant greater pain as he experienced the steady and inexorable decline of his physical health. On 31 July 1992, God called Leonard to himself. The motto of the Royal Air Force, *Per Ardua ad Astra*, sums up the arduous experiences of his life, before he took off on his last flight 'to the stars' to meet the God who made him.

# I

## Coming to terms
## with illness

*Leonard Cheshire with Her Majesty Queen Elizabeth, the Queen Mother at Le Court, Liss, Hants in 1955.*

# Reflections on the motor neurone disease

## June 1992

### Emptying the self

As you advance into this disease you feel your body getting weaker. You can do much less physically. You also find yourself carrying this tremendous weight of tiredness, so that it's an enormous effort to get started. Now this fact makes me think of two things.

Firstly, the most fundamental of all, the really important thing for us to do, is to empty ourselves, to encourage self-emptying. A Jesuit will talk about it as self-surrender.

But it is the emptying of everything self-centred, even if it is a good thing. Your attachment to earthly things is dissolved so that God can fill you totally.

If you read most of the theological books about our Lord you find that at the heart of it the writers are saying that his life consisted of total self-surrender, self-renunciation. So that is my first point. As your bodily faculties go, so you can remind yourself that that is just what you should be doing internally. In a curious way it helps you. I used to have an addiction to coffee and I knew that I really was hooked on coffee. If anybody said that they thought I should cut it down, I found a good reason for not doing so. But now coffee means nothing to me. I used to drink seven or eight cups a day and now I may just manage one and a half.

## Praying out the negatives

Secondly, an insight from the life of St Thérèse of Lisieux. Towards the end of her life she experienced a great tiredness because she had TB. She felt cold and weak. But every time she felt something like that she said, 'I'll offer it on behalf of a missionary somewhere who is too tired to make his next journey'. Now, that's a lovely thought and you can do that as well. You can say, 'Well, I'm just lying in bed here and I can offer it for my wife or for anybody close to me, for members of the Leonard Cheshire Foundation or even somebody I don't know at all'.

You feel that you are being given a wonderful opportunity for giving, in a more constructive way than when you had your full faculties about you. Well, I don't want to make comparisons because really you can't. You have no criteria with which to judge. But I still feel very deeply indeed that you can achieve more from the inside than you can from the outside. I feel this because when God came to save the world he didn't do it from the outside with the manifestation of an immense power, before which we would all have had to fall on our knees and agree. This would have been a form of compulsion. Rather he did it unseen and from the inside. No one saw his footprints and he is still doing it now all the time. This is what Jesus did. He worked from the inside not only in this world but in the world of the dead as well.

He entered the world of the dead. His work wasn't finished when he died on the Cross. We know that he reached even the most distant sinner, so that he could express a solidarity with every single person in the world no matter what his state. He did this in the hope of bringing them in as part of his Body, the mystical Body of Christ, his risen, glorified Body.

## Joy

So if that is the way that God works, then if you find yourself inside a disability, there must be ways in which you can work with (I don't like to say 'for') disabled people; ways which you can't actually describe or see; working in a more profound way than you could as a very fit man on the outside. That gives me great joy; a kind of joy that wants to well up inside me. I say that with hesitation because when my family look at me and obviously see me slipping away I must respond to their need and be careful not to sound unkind. But if it is joy within me, then in some way that I don't understand, it's going to be shared by those I'm close to. That is the most significant part of this disability to me.

## The inner reality

You ask is this the inner reality of the disability for me? I can only answer, yes, I think it is. You see, you are doing two things. Firstly, you're doing what you can to complete your duties, your external duties on earth; secondly, you are trying to spiritualise (if that is the right word), trying to complete the spiritual work that God has given you. Jesus invites us, as members of the Church which is his Body, to share in his redeeming of the world not only through the sacraments but in all its work properly undertaken, and through all its members. So you and I have a part in this, both for ourselves and for others, not through our own merits but uniting our efforts and suffering with those of our Saviour who died for us. I know one has to be careful saying that because you mustn't sound presumptuous, but it is true. St Paul said, 'It is now my joy to suffer for you; for the sake of Christ's Body, the Church, I am completing what still remains for Christ to suffer in my own person', but such participation presupposes a degree of spiritual maturity. So St Paul goes on to say that to make each one of you a mature member of Christ's Body, 'I am toiling strenuously with all the energy and power of Christ at work in me' (Col 1:24, 29).

Physical weakness helps you understand our total dependence on God. You and I see a picture of two people standing up in that photograph on the study wall: I can see they could stand up all day, and I now think how on earth could they do that. You see I can't stand for fifteen minutes before I begin to wilt. I feel my own weakness and I think, 'But God is sustaining the entire work, the entire cosmos'. And that is the least of his activities. He has been doing it ever since the beginning and will do it until the end. So we have the new heaven and the new earth; and what then? Somehow your own weakness makes you understand in a more realistic way the immense power of God; a power which is Love. This is very badly expressed but I am struggling to say something important.

Well, you are absolutely right when you say that you have been wondering whether my original assent to my condition was notional or real. At the beginning I just knew that *motor neurone* meant that you got weaker. My wife, Sue, explained what the disease was, as she had considerable experience with nursing other patients in her Homes, and she tried to keep me as composed as possible. I knew that there was no way out of it and that didn't bother me in the least. I completely accepted it. But as you go on you find that it brings physical problems. Some of these are quite obnoxious and painful: it stops you sleeping, your internal organs cease working in the way they should, and this is also true of your external organs. For example, you get surprised by cramp. One thing I am experiencing is quite severe cramp and you are surprised by that. But I find that is very, very healthy, because the moment it takes me by surprise it confronts me with reality.

This surprise makes me say, 'Were you just agreeing because you didn't understand what it really meant or are you agreeing with your whole person?' But then it very quickly makes me realise, 'Ah, I must take into account everything – no matter what is going to happen'. So now, I am much more in a frame of mind to expect all kinds of physical limitations and inconveniences. I don't think I quite expected it at the beginning. Now there may be a couple of minutes hesitation but no more than that.

## Religion and acceptance

Of course I have found with religion that it is very easy to say the things you know you ought to say but may not really be meaning them. I am very aware of the difference between the Greek concept of 'knowing' and the Jewish concept of 'knowing'. With the Jews, 'knowing' is assent with the whole of your being but for the Greeks it's merely intellectual assent. For instance when I became a Catholic you were taught always to say, 'I accept it'. Well that is just a phrase. You can easily say it, but even if you put it into more meaningful words you may be simply saying it in the intellect. I have recognised over the years that here lies a danger: I have seen other people say that and said to myself, 'Do they really mean it?'

## The genuine response

In fact I have argued that the person who is hit by a disaster, for example the loss of somebody very close to them or total disability received through an accident, and who really rebels may well be more genuine than the person who says 'I accept it. I offer it'. In the second case you can't tell that the person really means it. So it's interesting to me to discover that you noticed in me something I hadn't detected.

At the beginning I thought I had totally accepted it. But one or two people have said they wondered whether I really had. There must have been something about me that made you wonder that. I think it is true that as I've suddenly come up against a physical barrier I wasn't expecting I've begun to say, 'How am I going to cope with this?' Well, I shouldn't be saying that but it immediately made me realise that's a part of it and that makes it all the more meaningful.

Were it just a simple weakening and nothing else, you are not accepting very much. When you see for yourself what other people have got, e.g. in India, it is quite good for you. I think I have already said one of my difficulties is getting so thin that you get sore wherever you sit or lie. But then you look at the starving children and the starving old people lying and sitting on the floor. One never thinks of that. You just think, 'a little emaciated body'. But it's the same thing for them – 'pray for prisoners as if you were in prison yourself' (Heb 13:3). And when you pray for the starving you should try somehow to look at them and picture yourself like that. I retain my dignity and calm in the way that that little child or mother has, but what would I feel like, sitting on a stone floor all day with no flesh on me at all? So it is quite good for one.

# II

## The
## Family of the Cross

*Leonard Cheshire and his wife Sue (Lady Ryder) at Cavendish, Suffolk, 1975, where Cheshire died in 1992.*

# Reflections
## June 1992

### Origins/historical perspective

On the subject of the *Family of the Cross* I had a great desire during my time at Midhurst* to establish such a group. The world needs contemplatives but there are so many demands for the active life that there are fewer vocations to the contemplative Orders. But I realised there must be many disabled or sick people who have a call to be contemplatives but who can't join a monastery because of their condition. So, my idea

---

\* King Edward VII's Sanatorium for Officers, Midhurst.

then was to create a monastery, a Home, that was geared to look after disabled people where they can lead that life. I bought a piece of land outside Bethlehem with views of both Jerusalem and Bethlehem, intending it to be used for this monastery or Home. But it wasn't realistic. The monastic life centres round the Divine Office, recited and sung in a dignified way, and people with speech impediments or spasms would have great difficulty doing this.

Suddenly, the Family of the Cross took the form it has taken now: 'leave people where they are'. However, I wasn't a disabled person so I knew nothing about the problems of praying when you are disabled. I have read various books and selections from books by modern writers and they tend to say that when they are ill they are forced to focus all their energy on getting well – so they cannot pray. And that I think is the accepted practice. But when you look at our Lord, who took all our sufferings on himself and prayed all the time for sinners, it does seem to me that we are forced to try and do a little better than that.

## Emerging perspectives

What I am now finding is that concentrating the mind is difficult. It just wanders. I know one's mind wanders anyway but far more in this condition. You can be at Mass and suddenly a thought is sparked off and you follow it, to quickly end up miles away. You can lie quietly in bed intending to keep an hour's silence but just end up mentally floating around anywhere. So I would like to try and address this problem.

## A personal goal

My initial thinking is that each of us has a goal to go for – God has a plan for each of us. In broad terms we have some idea of what that plan is and what that goal is. I mean I know what some of my goals are: I started the Foundation, started Ryder-Cheshire, initiated the World Memorial Fund and therefore have a responsibility to help them on their way as best I can. Even if they were totally delegated, as the Leonard Cheshire Foundation is, I still have a role to play. I need to keep in personal contact, need to let them know that I am interested in them and am not forgetting them. I try to make any contribution that I can. So it seems to me that one line I can try and follow is to keep thinking of them during the day. For example I let my mind go to Port Elizabeth Cheshire Home, South Africa, where they have just taken the first black resident. That, of course was a very big thing for the white residents, who, for all these years have been looked after by black staff. They thought, so why don't we invite black residents? Well the first black resident has gone there and that is a great start.

Now, in thinking of these residents at the Port Elizabeth Home I already have a small image of them and, in fact, already you are saying a little prayer. I am continually struck by that line in Hebrews (13:3), 'Remember those who are in prison, as though you were in prison with them'. It convinces me that when we pray for people we shouldn't just pray for John Jones in an intellectual, abstract way. We should try and put ourselves imaginatively in his position, inviting him to enter the inner room of our heart and be present there along with all of us in the presence of God.

I am beginning to think that one way back from that woolly state I described earlier is to do this. It's no use trying to embark on long periods of concentrated prayer or even concentrated recollection. Better to work at these little spontaneous acts. Fr Bruno* said, 'Acts of Love'. I must find out more of what that is.

## A means not an end

Obviously prayer is a means to an end and not an end in itself. In the Family of the Cross we adopt the prayer of silence. This prayer of silence is a means towards an end and if we find that we can't keep it in that form then let's change the form. I think individual members should be free to do that. It is very easy to get trapped into systems of prayer that you have been trained in. I think that looking at the whole of life even the best people can confuse the means for the end. With the Jews the Law was

---

* Carthusian Monk of Parkminster Abbey, Sussex.

33

everything; in the Catholic Church you can end up saying, 'I'm a member of the Church, I go to the sacraments, I'm all right'. This is to forget that the sacraments are merely there to assist the re-creation of yourself into the new person you have got to be.

## The partnership with God

The spiritual life I would describe as a partnership with God on your journey through life. We can only achieve our particular goal if God gives us the directions and the driving power. The great advantage of the prayer of silence is that it allows God to work in you – inside you – in a way that he can't when you are active. I mean he is working inside us all the time but in different ways according to what room we ourselves give him.

I think that one of the major difficulties with the prayer of silence is the fact that you are surrounded at all times by a certain number of problems, things that have gone wrong. You get a letter about something and you are sorry about it. Now the danger is that you let these things run round your mind to no actual purpose. You are not actually working on them saying, 'What shall I do?'. You are just letting them fill your mind. I cannot accept that all we have to do in this situation is just carry on and be told that your life is a life of prayer. It does seem to me that we are obliged to make a positive move to push them out.

## A new discipline

When I took on the Memorial Fund I realised that I virtually had two full-time jobs and that I couldn't afford to carry any single load that was not necessary. I mean not doing engagements that were unnecessary but also not carrying interior loads that were unnecessary. So I made a practice that whenever a thought came to me, say a slight niggle or a feeling of annoyance at what somebody had done, I'd immediately refer it back to God and refuse to let it in at all. If I got a brilliant new idea that would change the whole world I again refused to look at it and I'd give it back to God. I'd ask God to take it from me with the knowledge that if it was something meant to be it would come back in a refined form.

Now, so long as I kept that up it was a great, great help. It makes it easier to sleep, because when you lie down to sleep things begin to come into your mind and you are able to push them straight back out. So I do think that this is also a little discipline that one can start. I know it mustn't be done with great determination and tension but rather with a gentle discipline. Otherwise it is easy just to fritter your day away and neither relax nor work. You end up doing nothing constructive, you are just loitering.

One thing bothers me slightly. The way Fr John came here, out of the blue, makes it obvious to me that his arrival was meant to be. Therefore I also know he has something to tell me as well as giving the sacraments. But when I ask him about prayer he brushes it aside. He says, 'You are who you are. God is who God is and he lives in you, so you don't need to think about prayer'. I ask him to give me some little further insight but he doesn't. Now, in making just that statement I am left feeling quite strongly that he has something to tell me. So, in the last day or two, I thought to myself, 'let me look at you from a different point of view'.

## Prayer and work – two means to one end

I have already said that prayer is a means to an end and not an end in itself. Now each of us has received work given to us to do by God. At the end of his life Jesus said, 'I have finished the work that you gave me to do' (Jn 17:4). That same statement also applies to everyone of us and our work is at different levels. It involves our daily work from a human point of view, but it is also a spiritual work in the sense of co-operating with God in creating the new man. We are here for a purpose and the all-important thing is crossing that finishing line.

## Final perseverance and final priorities

The Church urges final perseverance, but we all run a race. It's no use running the race brilliantly and then stopping one yard short. You have to cross that tape. If we take it that all of us (but I am really talking about me) have got work to do then I need to know what are the priorities of that work still outstanding, and I have to do my utmost to complete it. In order to do so I need prayer. I need prayer to help me to know what it is to be open and sensitive to good inspirations of the Holy Spirit. I need to be able to discern in the moments of daily life what is, as it were, a call from God, a nudge from God. I need to discern what is necessary and what is unnecessary. So, if we look at prayer from that point of view and not just as prayer then perhaps it takes on new dimensions. If we look at my particular work, I started Homes for disabled people; I helped to start the Ryder-Cheshire project, the Mission, I started the Memorial Fund and I have a family. Clearly I have a duty to all those aspects to carry on to the very end fulfilling that personal duty. If I start from that point and then look at prayer in relation to these aspects of my life then maybe it takes on a new significance.

## Present realities

To repeat once again – my mind is woolly. It is difficult to hold it down on to something. Even dictating a letter, I now have great difficulty focusing my mind on the letter although it is quite specific and held in front of me. This also happens to me at Mass. My hour of prayer in the morning, the time I used to really love, is now just sitting and finding I'm all over the place.

As my complaint takes a greater hold on me I get forgetful. The fact that I can't remember Carney's name – Christian name – is astonishing. But I am finding it all the time. I was speaking to Lynette, who has worked for us for twelve years as International Secretary and I suddenly forgot her name. So I am experiencing a woolliness, a lack of concentration and a growing forgetfulness.

I still hold an insight that came to me forty years ago in Midhurst when I had TB: I saw it was necessary to use the events of your daily life to be led into prayer. Perhaps I thought about stupid things. For example, when you go through a front door just reflect briefly that one day, please God, we will walk through the front door of Heaven, or when the telephone goes, offer a short prayer for the person you are going to speak to: the briefest of prayers for saying the right thing. A telephone call could thus be another symbol of a little inward prompting from the Holy Spirit. You can look at it in many different ways.

## Praying for the Homes

I now have Homes in fifty countries. I used to sit down for half an hour and in my mind just go round to all of them. I would briefly bring them to mind, just a little mental picture. I didn't speak to them, didn't involve them in conversation but in a manner of speaking just invited them in to sit with me in the inner room of my heart in the presence of God. I found that very meaningful. It was not just that I felt I was saying a prayer for them, or even because I was inviting them to sit in the presence of God with me, but rather that it actually gave me strength. Being able to picture them in my imagination made them come to life. Then, briefly, I thought of all the things they had done and the struggle they had been through, and it strengthened me. Now I cannot do that systematically, but throughout the day I continually feel I need to keep doing it. I go to South Africa, go to Australia, to South America, Canada and picture the Homes briefly. That in itself is a prayer. I mean it as a prayer, not as a mere mental exercise. Our prayer needs to embrace the whole world; it's not a selfish thing. We need to pray to be responsive to the word of God; but that is not our main prayer.

## Present priorities

If you look through the Old Testament nearly all the prayers are for other people, for one's nation. Therefore, I feel that that is one important thing: remembering people. The other thing is – what work have I still to do? Completing the work for the Italian version of my book, *Where is God in all this?*, is certainly a priority, I think. I also realise that I mustn't make a mistake and devote too much energy to that because then I won't have the energy for something of greater importance. The Leonard Cheshire Foundation is virtually delegated, the structure is all in place. There are still things that need a little bit of direction and I have to make certain that the right Committee is formed to supervise the total delegation which has already been formed. I need to pass on a few views to them.

I need personal contact. I keep thinking I must ring Eliza Braye in South Africa just as I used to. Last night Jake Newham rang me from Canberra. He is now our National Chairman of Ryder-Cheshire, Australia, and ex-Chief of the Air Staff. He's a lovely man and what he has done, especially for the New Guinea Home, is quite phenomenal. He has said that he is going to ring me every week or two and that in itself is a wonderful contact.

You ask am I a perfectionist. Do I cross the t's and dot the i's? You suggest that this can be a good thing but that it also involves the danger of tiring oneself. In my view it's not good enough to give anything less than everything in order to live the life that we think God wants us to live. I can't accept anything less than that. I certainly don't mean I reach it but there must be a goal.

## Praying the Homes

I can't honestly say I find this prayer tiring. I actually find it the opposite. I find a sense of relief, a sense of happiness in having made that contact. I picture the Cheshire Home at Regina or the Cheshire Home in Vancouver for head injuries, a very difficult form of disability to look after. The fact that I have visited them by way of thought and prayer gives me a real joy. If I am just lying down, my mind idling, I feel a little uncomfortable and uneasy.

You see, ever since the Carthusians taught me the silent prayer I've moved away from the more Jesuit form of prayer in which you use your mind to picture an episode in the gospels in order to prepare yourself for prayer. I now find that method very tiring because my mind is working all day, or trying to work and the last thing I want to do when I come to prayer is to use my mind. I am criticised by some for this but I do feel that the Western Church may be slightly over-influenced by the Greeks. The Church used Greek philosophy as its vehicle for transmitting its message and I think that Plotinus, the neo-Platonist, had an influence on St Augustine and thus the mind came a bit too much into his prayer. I say this with humility.

It is not my mind that I want to use. As

Fr Bruno says, it's an act of love. Thus, joining myself to Katpadi, the Cheshire Home for leprosy patients, South India, is an act of love. I mean, when you think of your brother, your father or your son it cannot be understood as a mental exercise that tires you, but rather as a bond of love.

## Desk work

The point you raise about desk work; that is crucial. I still don't know how much effort I should devote to that and how much I should just let go. My conflict is that I pick up a letter from somebody who has done a lot for me and of whom I am very fond – they have written to me and I just feel I must answer. But yet I can't do too many. Once you start it escalates. So, I recognise that is one area where I need counselling and you will be one who can counsel me, because as you are one of those who are doing it, then you are given the grace to decide right. Also I think I need to say little prayers about it. Not long prayers, as it's enough that the thought is in your mind. When we don't know what prayer to offer or how to pray as we ought, the Holy Spirit, through our inarticulate groans is pleading for us (Rom 8:26), because he knows the mind of God, and therefore I realise it's enough to have the desire there for it to become a prayer. But I still need to avoid this idling of the mind into all sorts of nothingness. I am glad that Sue, my wife, continues over the years to build up the spiritual life in her Foundation so that when the time comes for her to hand over, or die, the Sue Ryder Foundation may not be run only by professionals or as a caring business. It depends on people who pray and meet in the Sue Ryder Prayer Fellowship and go on short Retreats. I do so hope this will consolidate and grow for her sake and all that she is involved in, both now and in the years which lie ahead.

## The journey

I want to go back to the question of acceptance. I think we can agree that life is a journey, of many different sorts and kinds, that all combine to make the one total journey. When we have a new job we take it on, although we don't see where it is leading us. When we are given something special to do by God, if we saw what was coming very likely we'd say NO at the beginning. But he just shows us the first few steps; we accept them and we go, and we meet many surprises on the way. Some surprises we accept very gracefully and positively. Others we possibly don't accept at all. When it comes to something like being told you've got a given disability, in my case I feel quite certain I accepted it. It was just another thing that happened in life. But clearly I didn't know in my own mind all that was going to happen. Cardinal Newman puts it well, 'I do not ask to see the distant scene; one step enough for me'.

## The example of our Lord

I am sure that our Lord did not know at the beginning everything that his vocation was going to involve. It was real to him more and more as his life unfolded. He would have known a great deal but clearly he was going to see it unfold in greater detail. The fact that he was crushed in the garden of

Gethsemane means that there must have been something there he wasn't quite prepared for. As I put earlier in my book I am convinced that it was the fact of 'becoming sin' (2 Cor 5:21). He not only carried our sins (1 Pet 2:22) but, in a way beyond our understanding, he became sin personified that in him we might share in God's righteousness (cf 2 Cor 5:21; Gal 3:13). It would seem that he was removed from any realisation of the presence of God. The cry of Jesus on the Cross (Mt 27:46) sums this up, 'My God, my God, why have you forsaken me?'; abandonment, that is, not in fact but in perception.

## Acceptance

There is a great danger that we automatically say what we know we ought to say. Forty years ago the Church was always telling you – if anything disastrous happens – to say 'I accept it' or 'I offer it up'. And so it's quite easy to make that an automatic response which isn't really in your heart. Let me look at my own case. In the four or five months since I've known the diagnosis I've been going down more or less steadily and I do find new things I wasn't expecting. Things that limit your privacy, your ability to manage on your own. I have no doubt that some of those are going to be difficult to accept. All the same, in your heart, you know perfectly well that it's uniting you a little more closely with the sufferings of our Lord. It's bringing you closer to other disabled people. They are going through it but we look at them and I don't think we really always appreciate what some of the things they have to put up with mean to them as people. You see, some disabling diseases, for instance, produce far more saliva than you can either swallow or actually spit out. So when we see people like that perhaps we don't think how embarrassed they must feel. They can't explain it; that would be beside the point. They can't even talk properly. But little things like that take on a fuller meaning and understanding. It's actually quite helpful being in that position and being able to go through it yourself, because you do see it in a way that you hadn't thought of before. It is common for patients suffering with Motor Neurone Disease to have an excess of saliva but I am an exception. Sue cannot obtain from anywhere a remedy which induces saliva, having tried countless pharmacists. My mouth is dry and very sore and despite all that Sue does, she feels she has failed me.

## The central spiritual insight

I still come back to that all-pervading thought that the more you suffer physical disability or any physical impairment the more you can use it to understand your spiritual weakness. I'm finding that confirmation of my prayer for the Homes is a great help. It's something you can focus on and something solid you can hold on to when you are in a sort of flux and sinking, as it were, into depths with no foothold. From it you also find other similar things which provide support .

## Willpower and energy

If we are going to complete the work we have been given to do we need to have the willpower and the energy to do it, don't we?

So, first thing in the morning I try and say a little prayer asking for the willpower and energy and making a good resolution. It's things like that, which relate either to your work, the people you're fond of, the needs of the world, or your own particular needs from hour to hour, that give you a basis for prayer.

It's no use trying to plan routines or develop systems; you won't succeed. If I try that approach I end up thinking that it's hopeless and all I've got to do is think about getting better and relax. You've got to keep trying to find the mean between the two and the solution lies in the little things, I think. It's like forming a habit. You do something once, you then do it twice, you do it three times and it begins to get easier. Then it begins to become natural to you. But if you let it go altogether then it's very difficult to recover.

## Prayer directions

In conversation with Fr John, some days ago, I said that I didn't really understand what he was saying. Now I think he didn't actually understand my question. I suspect that he supposed I was asking about some great system of prayer, some sort of essential and basic instruction on prayer. But all I wanted was a little pointer.

At our next meeting I told him again how woolly my thoughts are. I told him how difficult it is to concentrate on even doing a letter and that I can't accept anything less than doing your best, not only in your daily work and in all your responsibilities but also in the spiritual life as well.

We are told to keep our minds fixed on the things in heaven and not on the things of earth. St James says that he who gazes steadily at the perfect law of freedom and acts accordingly will be blessed (1:25). At this point in my life there must be something to strive for.

The prayer that I always used to make, going round each of the Cheshire Homes one by one is, I think, already discussed in the book *Where is God in all this*? I just picture them briefly and, so to speak, invite them to come with me into the inner room of my heart where God lives in each of us and just being quietly present there together. I am greatly influenced by that phrase towards the end of Hebrews (13:3) that says 'pray for prisoners as if you were in prison yourself'. Well, now I understand this to mean that instead of praying for John Jones just as John Jones, I have rather to put myself in his place, picture his predicament, his environment. So in my mind I start in Capetown with the Cheshire Home for whites. I just briefly picture them as if I were there. I don't linger there nor do I enter into a conversation with them but I can actually picture them. Then I move on to the Home for coloureds in Capetown and so I work my way round the world ending up in Southern Ireland, in Cork. I find that a most meaningful prayer. For one thing it strengthens the bond between us and also seems to give me strength. Since I'm primarily responsible for the Cheshire Homes, for their coming into being (though other people have actually done the work), obviously I feel not only a continuing love for them but also a responsibility for them. If I can't visit in person at least I can visit in this way.

Now I can no longer do the half-hour in one period that I used to do but I can make a point whenever the thought comes to me of doing that with one or two Cheshire Homes. That is something I can hold on to and build upon. I can also extend it to other things as well: to abortion, to problems in the world (like Yugoslavia), to my family and friends. Obviously my family comes into it even more than the Homes.

I put my experience in prayer once more to Fr John. He said: 'That's an excellent way of prayer. You concentrate on that.' He was very brief, didn't waste a word and just wanted to move on and not take my time or tire me. It really was most helpful.

## An international homes route

When we pray, our prayer needs to embrace the whole world, doesn't it? Yes, we pray for ourselves but somehow our prayer needs to extend out to the whole human family. I think the basic principle, when you are in this sort of woolly state and you have difficulty keeping to a routine, is not to aim too high. Just take little things that you can hold on to and build on them. As you start the habit, every now and then it will gradually build up. In my case, I may move to a Cheshire Home in South America. Instead of your thoughts going uselessly all round the place they gradually become more focused.

Yes, I do have a complete international route and it's something ingrained in me. I have only to put myself into one Cheshire Home or Ryder-Cheshire Home for it to lead me automatically to the next. I start in South Africa, work my way across to Namibia then up the west coast and on into Europe; across to Moscow, back down eastern central Europe, Bethlehem, East Africa, India and Ceylon. From there I go to Malaysia, Singapore, Bangkok and Indonesia. Working my way round the Philippines and on to Japan, Hong Kong and China I come down to Papua – New Guinea, round Australia and on to New Zealand. Then I go to Vancouver, and across Canada before working my way down the United States and the Caribbean, to South America. I then come to Penzance here, to work my way up England, Wales and Scotland and then across to Northern Ireland, Dublin and the Irish Homes.

## Motor neurone reflections

A small point about motor neurone. I said that it was difficult to sleep. The reason is you get peculiar cramps which at night are hard to bear. I know this is really irrelevant because it happens to so many people. I find it impossible to lie at ease in bed due to the fact that I have only one lung and that I now have no flesh on my body. But the basic problem with it – to me – is the fatigue. There is just this weight of heaviness and tiredness, both mental and physical, so sleep makes a big difference. Obviously eating is important but it's difficult to eat as I can't tolerate too much and now have swallowing problems. Then you must exercise within your limits as much as you can but you can't go beyond the limits. Doing letters, seeing people and talking is tiring, so it's very difficult to work out the right balance of what you should do to remain at your optimum. In a way it's quite a challenge; I find it exhilarating in one sense but nobody can give you a straight answer. You have to work it out yourself.

## The spiritual side

I come now to the spiritual side. It makes you think by analogy of the effect of sin on our spirit. Sin must impose a weight – in fact some of the spiritual writers talk about the weight of sin. Apart from clouding your judgement it does weigh you down. So, all these things, if you can use them as analogies to look at the spiritual life, really are a great blessing and also another entry into prayer. Therefore I am gradually finding that my physical condition as it deteriorates can be a real help to my spiritual life. When I was doing the Anglia Television interview they asked me a question about death. I think they were really saying, 'Are you looking forward to it?' Well I had to say that, first, I cannot bring myself to think about heaven. By this I mean that the thought of what God is giving us is so overwhelming that you just can't face it. It's too unbelievable. Then immediately it induces a thought that if this is what God is giving us, out of his sheer goodness and not for any merit at all of mine, then 'please give me a little more time to do better than I have done'.

## A new order of being

There are so many things to be done. There are your friends whom you want to be with and your family whom you don't want to leave. That may be a selfish side but my answer would be that I'd prefer to stay on the battlefield of life rather than leave it earlier than I've got to. I think you are torn in two directions. You are brought back to that earlier point once again – final perseverance and the fact that Jesus said 'I have finished the work that you gave me to do' (Jn 17:4). Clearly each of us has to finish the work we've been given. Any thought of 'Oh yes, the end has come, that's wonderful, I'll just move into God's house', as many people put it, which is entirely true and legitimate, must also be balanced I think by the other. I like very much St Thérèse's statement: 'I want to spend my heaven doing good on earth'. We need to see not just that we are part of the whole human family but that there is no break between this world and the next. Obviously it's a totally different kind of world, a new order of existence but it is still the one creation of God. I still think the best analogy of all is the seed. The seed and the flower. You look at that rotten little nothing; who could ever imagine it was going to become a beautiful flower. And that is so with us. We are the seed now and we will be the flower in heaven. This is such an overwhelming thought that I find you can't really let your thoughts dwell on it. You know it but then put it to one side.

## Longing for Heaven

You mention that some people throughout their lives have a deep longing for death so that they can be in heaven and that's completely understandable and right. But I think we all know that our heaven is related in one sense to what we do here on earth. We don't go to heaven by any merit of our own but we are constantly told that your reward in heaven will be great. The sufferings that you've borne patiently or the punishments you have suffered, for no good reason, the way that you love your neighbour and God, the fact that you work for the good of other people, all this and more will mean that your reward will be great. There is that perpetual paradox in the Christian life: on the one hand God's sheer goodness takes us to heaven not because we are good or have contributed anything; on the other hand Jesus says, whoever gives a cup of water to the least of these brethren of mine has given it to me and of such is the Kingdom of Heaven. It's just perpetual paradox. I think you need the two, side by side. You need the longing for heaven but you also need a similar longing to run the full course on earth. We need to miss no opportunity of leading our life to the full (in the good sense) as we should.

## The Mass

This brings me back to Arthur in the early part of the book.* I quoted him as saying, 'Ah, the peace after hearing Mass'. To Fr John, the centre of everything is the Mass and he says it in a very beautiful way. You can see his whole heart is in it and I find now that I am coming back to that fact in

---

* Arthur Dykes, Leonard's first patient at his Home, Le Court, Liss, Hants, see *Where is God in all this?* p.33.

the sense of seeing it as the centre of the day and the centre of one's prayer. In fact I suppose theologically the Mass is the centre of the Church. It's the Mass that brings the great mystery of Christ's redemption of the world present today. And it's through – (perhaps this is something only for believers) through eating his Body and drinking his Blood that not only are we given everlasting life but we become part of his Body and he enters us.

Consequently if one's prayer in the day was orientated towards being ready for Mass and an act of thanksgiving for the Mass, that in itself would be very meaningful. The Mass is something going on that you can take part in, that you can see and that you are sharing with others. What matters for me is the Mass, because it was at the Last Supper that we all became part of the Mystical Body.

## Prayer developments

Going back to the question of praying and the difficulty that I had earlier, it has all come completely right. When Fr John said, 'Yes, I like that idea of the way you pray for your Homes', I started doing that and found that it built up and up. It came more naturally to me during the day. Then I was able to speak to Fr Bruno on the 'phone because he is in hospital. I told him of this development and he said 'Yes'. He expanded on it, but afterwards I remarked to him: 'You said to me, "make acts of love". Could you please be more precise as to what you mean?' He replied 'Yes, I think of all the ways the good Lord has helped you. The things that you've done. You were a leader in the war, were able to achieve things in the war. You have done your work with the Cheshire Homes. People have helped you, pray for them then in this way. Thank the Lord, go over your life and pray in a prayerful way'.

Now I find that very helpful because it has reminded me of a lot of people I should be praying for, even people in the past I've not previously prayed for. So I feel more and more my present life should be spent that way because it is peaceful. Dictating letters gets tiring, my voice gives out, moving about is tiring, even just listening in conversations with people can be tiring. Hence I feel that even though I have a major problem in one of the projects affecting me I should still let it go. There are so many quotations in the Psalms: 'Unload your worries on the Lord and he will take care of them for you'. I think I must do that and I am finding that form of prayer very helpful. It makes me feel more peaceful. If I find myself awake at night because the dry throat and other things keep waking me I just peacefully do that and go off to sleep again. It's not easy to let things go though; people mean a lot to you. You think, 'I must just answer that letter to this person', but once you start doing that where do you stop?

## An insight

Yes, it's a development and an insight. Fr Bruno is in hospital and he said: 'Are you able to read?' I replied: 'To tell you the truth, no. I find that I pick something up and I can't follow it'. He said: 'I'm just the same', and he is a tremendous spiritual reader. He said: 'I can't concentrate enough to read it'. Then he said: 'That's the prayer I'm using'. I find the fact that Fr Bruno finally approved this type of intercessory prayer very supportive and encouraging. I am also helped by the passage in Hebrews (13:3): 'Pray for those in prison, as if you were in prison yourself'. In other words put yourself in their shoes, not by using your mind but by just identifying with them in imagination in the presence of God. Fr Bruno takes it a step further and I find that it fits.

## The future path

Yes, I think that from a spiritual point of view that is the way I should go and also there's the future to pray about. I mean I don't want to leave too heavy a burden for Sue (Lady Ryder) and I want to do everything I can to ease that burden now and for the future. So there is that also to pray for. Hence I feel peaceful and as the weeks go on I am going to get more and more insights into this.

# III

## *Leave-taking*

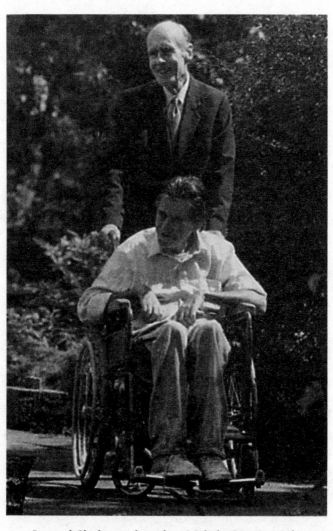

*Leonard Cheshire with resident, Malcolm Stewart, at the*
*Cheshire Home, Mayfield House, Edinburgh, 1990.*

# July 1992

## Midhurst.
## The Family of the Cross

Forty years ago, when I was at Midhurst, the idea first came to me to establish this group (see p.29). I started with the basic thought of an hour of silence – silent prayer. I didn't give much thought to how disabled people with a heavy disability could manage to pray in this way. I did not envisage the difficulties they might have but now that I am one of them myself I am beginning to see.

## Personal experience

In order to establish the hour of prayer in my own life I gave up the rosary. I decided in place of the rosary I'd do the equivalent of thirty minutes of silent prayer until it became established and then I'd bring back the rosary. I did this because I find in prayer you have to move step by step; and that was how it worked. Then, year by year, the thirty minutes became longer and longer. Thus, I think that is a first principle, that if you want to adopt a new or different form of prayer and you don't have the free space to do it then substitute for it something that is already a habit, because if it has become a habit it will come back.

## A point of dispute

As I have said before, nearly everybody, all the priests and the modern spiritual writers, say that when you are ill all your energies are focused on coping with your illness and getting better, so you cannot pray. But I dispute that. I know it's true but I refuse to accept that we should just merely resign ourselves to that. We should find a way of making our time prayerful. In my case I found that instead of the hour of silence, which I can't keep because my thoughts are too woolly, I devote much more time to praying for the Homes in the way I used to. That has become my habit. It is something concrete I can hold on to. My mind can go to Turfhall, the Home for coloureds in Cape Town. I can briefly picture them, almost feel I am there, but I do so having put myself consciously in the presence of God. So I am inviting them to join me. We sit together and we mutually support each other.

## Praying for the Homes

Now that is something that I know and am used to, something concrete and something which I enjoy. I mustn't take this too literally but the Homes are for me similar to a member of the family, like my children. I don't say that as if they were my children but I am talking about the nature of the relationship. So I enjoy it. Furthermore I feel it is a projection of my work but, whereas

I can't be writing them letters very easily, certainly can't visit them, can't take part in committee meetings about them, I can do this. Now as I do this it is beginning to make me feel that it is not enough just to picture them. You need to be in the attitude of mind where you know that your prayers advance you towards a goal.

All the Cheshire Homes have to improve, they have to become better established. My idea is that once they have reached their maximum point they should be reaching out towards some other service to the community. So they need a dynamic element to their growth and that should come into your prayer. You should be praying that they get the strength to go on and on and on, improving both the quality of life within the Home and extending the help they can give, but also realising more and more that all of us must work for the common good of the whole of the human family. That brings in another element to your prayer: famine, trouble spots in the world, human rights violated. You can hold on to those and bring them in too.

## Encouraging signs

This is going to sound a little presumptuous but I'll explain it when I have said it. Several things have happened that have given me immense encouragement in this. There is a Cheshire Home in the Algarve, in Portugal, that received a grant from government to build, and an English lady living down there accepted this and started building a very prestigious Home. The grant was then cut off; the building was about a quarter up, with no roof. It was just a shell. It looked as if they would never get the money and it was just deteriorating for everybody who drove along the road to look at. Four days ago I got a letter saying that the grant is being reinstated and it so happened that three nights previously I had been dwelling on it. Now it obviously wasn't my prayer that had achieved this, but it somehow brought the two together.

## The United Nations role

On the world stage the big thing I was working for, and getting myself geared for, was an enhanced UN role; in co-ordinating disaster relief, in being given the authority and teeth where human rights are grossly violated somewhere in the world and the government doing nothing about it (or maybe even causing it) to step in and stop it. With the Super-Power confrontation gone, that becomes a possibility because it has got to be a Security Council resolution. I was thinking of Africa but it would have been more sensible to think of Europe because we are on home ground, so to speak, and, to an African, a white military presence could be off-putting. I have made two trips to the UN to discuss this. I found great support amongst the officials concerned, especially Marrack Goulding, ex Foreign Office. He was one of the negotiators in Yugoslavia and it was discussing this with him that put up another idea concerning aid. When aid is going into a starving country, torn by civil war, send in soldiers in blue berets, ideally from the big powers which carry more muscle, as armed escorts.

## Sunday trading

I fought hard in the House of Lords against the ruling that the Government would not help local authorities prosecute traders that were breaking the law (it's a bit more complicated than that, but they wouldn't) and they refused to take any action themselves or even express a point of view. But the other day that was overruled and local authorities now do have the power and the backing to prosecute. Well, again, it wasn't my poor prayers, but the fact is that in different areas, since being withdrawn from action and now only being able to operate through prayer, and maybe offering the inconveniences of life, to see that something is happening is an encouragement. I feel that God is being good enough to give me those little pointers to say that this is the way you should work.

## Family of the Cross

So that leads me to think that if that is so for myself, why don't I start to put down some thoughts for disabled members of *The*

*Family of the Cross.* Cardinal Hume was adamant that it should be confined to disabled people but agreed it could be extended to those who help in some substantial way. If I were to try and do that in the next newsletter, it would be a starting point. We could then get some reactions back – because I think that people do find the hour of silence difficult.

The Family of the Cross needn't necessarily begin with an hour of silence. I mean that is the objective, but it may be that stage one, your initiation, so to speak, is a different form of prayer which each person can choose, dependent upon his past prayer life. Because this is what I think the lesson is: if you have a formed habit of prayer use that as the anchor to start praying in a different kind of way once you are ill or disabled. By disabled I mean a disability that affects your whole being, not just two of your limbs.

## New directives and understandings

Another little advance: I found that having got back into the habit of roaming round all the Homes first thing in the morning,

once I have woken up – or half woken up –
I say to myself, a new day is dawning. I
think: all over the world the Homes are
getting ready for their day's work and may
they all have a good day. May they all have
a sense of purpose because that is one thing
we must never lose.

Everybody is different. If I am just a sweep
and do nothing other than sweep and clean
the roads, that still is an important goal.
You've got goals of different types at different
levels of your life. But to achieve any of them
you need a sense of purpose. Your life mustn't
float about without any control. So, that I
find helpful. It helps me too, in my day. I feel
that week by week, my ideas may crystallise
a little more; some will be quite wrong but
others may be helpful.

## A changed involvement

The truth is that I have to withdraw from
active participation in all my ventures. I
have to do this as quickly as possible but
remain consistent in doing it properly. In
other words I have to see that the right
people are in place with the right instruc-

tions, or, according to which is appropriate, the correct vision of what we are going for. But that does not mean that my involvement diminishes – it just alters. I have to work for mutual goals in a different way. In fact it is true throughout the whole of life that if something happens to stop you doing your work or going for your target in the way that you have been doing, then it becomes necessary to work out a different way of doing so.

## Spiritual involvement

In my position at the moment the only way that I can work in all my ventures, the only way that I can continue contributing towards the development of different projects is to do so spiritually. In fact this gives me an ideal opportunity. The one hope is that I won't fall short. I obviously will fall short but I hope not too much. The obvious, principal way of involvement is prayer. I don't mean my old, lengthy set prayers, spoken prayers or any particular systematic way of praying. But I need to try to turn my life and the physical difficulties I have into a prayer. I think that means starting with what St Augustine defines as the prayer of desire. Thus your whole being, heart and mind, needs to be orientated towards God. If you start that way, then throughout the day you can bring in different people, different Homes, different problems into your thoughts while you are, so to speak, in a prayerful state of mind.

## Prayer of intercession

Earlier in these reflections I spoke about how difficult it is to concentrate the mind. Consequently you fall back on ways of praying that you were used to formerly. Ways that come easily. And a particular way for me is the prayer of intercession - because I can picture in my mind a Home. This is something I can hold on to.

## The Homes

Now as you move in mind or imagination – or whatever the right word is – through the Homes, you also cross areas of the world where there are problems, famine, civil strife in Somalia, the United Nations struggling to be more effective and so you can wander off and pray for these issues too.

## The new day

I find that the beginning of the day as you wake up is important. You are waking up to a new day. Picture in your mind in a very general way a whole world waking up with you. People are getting organised to go out to their work: some of them are leaders of government, others are going to sweep the streets, others, ill or disabled are at home. But there in that moment you have the whole world waking up, we hope to put the day to the best advantage.

The morning light is brushing aside the night's darkness. That also symbolises the fact that just as we are all in a state of becoming and evolving, so God is at work all the time, recreating the present earth and heaven into the new heaven and the new earth. So that process is also going on: identify with it.

Don't try to be clever and think it out – just have that thought in your mind. Beauty is springing out of darkness. As the darkness goes the light draws forth beauty in the same way that God's holy Spirit is working in us. If we allow him freedom, he is going to bring out a beauty in our lives. A beauty of a completely different kind. There are all sorts of ways and all sorts of areas of which this is one. You can turn your day quite joyfully and peacefully into a prayer. Once you begin the process using the things that you see and experience, you know these can be a means of reaching through to the spiritual dimension Somebody once said: 'the things that we see help us understand the unseen things.' I like the linking of what we do and what we see with a prayer aimed at the spiritual counterpart:

*'The shining sun looks down on all things and the work of the Lord is full of his glory'.*

Ecclesiasticus, 42:16

# Epilogue

Not long before Leonard became incapacitated by his illness, he invited me to supper at his apartment in Maunsel Street, London. Instead of talking about the Homes he had founded, as I rather expected, Leonard produced a little book and asked me if I had read it. I had. The title is *The Cry of Jesus on the Cross* ('My God, my God, why have you forsaken me' [Mt 27:46; Mk 15:34]). This cry, says the author, expresses the greatest loneliness imaginable, the experience of the absence of God, (p.64). Not something, one might think, that the Son of God could undergo. Nevertheless, he chose to be tempted (Heb 4:15) in *every* way that we are, though without sin. Leonard was greatly moved by this thought and its consequences for us. Our response, he said, must be to give nothing less than everything in return (see p.42.)

R.C.F.